CU00894693

Diary
Of
A
New
Referee

Fez Barnard

Diary of a New Referee

Second Edition
3rd December 2011

Copyright

Fez Barnard

ISBN 978-1-4710-4822-7

Published by

LULU.COM

Diary of a New Referee

From child abuse to foul and offensive language, the referee has to deal with it all. Standing in the middle of the park on your first game is daunting, especially when all eyes are looking at you, just waiting for you to make your first mistake. Inspired by Graham Poll and help from Tim Lawrence and Brian Hall, this diary provides an insight to problems and issues I had on the field of play and where I turned to enhance my knowledge. Hearing how others dealt with certain situations helped me enormously, I just hope my experiences can help you with your tricky situations.

Fez Barnard

Diary of a New Referee

All events detailed within are from recollection and published without malice. All persons, places, dates, teams and individuals have been altered. It is the event that is being used as an example.

All characters appearing in this work are fictitious and any resemblance to real persons, living or dead are purely coincidental.

Diary of a New Referee

Contents

Preface.

Over the years I have asked, pestered and cajoled by many people for information and explanations about the laws of the game. Such as '**What do I do if a mum shouts at her son**?', or '**When do I blow the final whistle**?', and so on. I thought it was about time that I gave something back to the game with the possibility of helping some new referees.

But before we continue, I would like to express my thanks to the following for their input and guidance over the years.

Julie
My beloved wife who provided understanding and a shoulder to cry on.

Martin
Who volunteered me to become a referee.

Joshua
My son, who dragged me to every game.

Tim Lawrence
For providing such enlightening courses.

Mike Smith
For such a brilliant radio show - Surrey Soccer at Brooklands FM.

Brian Hall
For detailed understanding of the finer points of the game.

Graham Poll
For inspiration to write this diary in the first place.

Darren Cullum & Richard Melinn
For the most fabulous podcast dealing with referees issues.

Mike Bull
For being a great mentor in the early days.

Sutton RA
For their guidance and numerous discussions.

Kings

For allowing me to referee. What a great bunch of lads.

Introduction.

The following pages take me back to my early days as an FA qualified referee, officiating grassroots youth football just as the FA brought out the respect campaign. I wrote this diary to provide an insight for new referees coming through the system in the hope that sharing some of my experiences would provide some help and guidance.

Standing in the middle of the park on your first game is daunting, especially when all eyes are looking at you, just waiting for you to make your first mistake.

The following pages provide an insight to problems and issues I had on the field of play and where I turned to enhance my knowledge. Hearing how others dealt with situations helped me enormously, I just hope my experiences can help you in your tricky situations.

Diary of a New Referee

Put my hand up.

Way back in 2006 my little 6 year lad wanted to start playing football for a club, with his friends George and Archie. Archie's dad Martin had been looking around for some time, and believed the level of grassroots football was not so good. So he asked, if any kids wanted to play football, they were to meet up at the local park on Saturday morning. Many kids turned up and Martin started testing them. Now that had a team, he needed a referee and asked for volunteers. No one put their hand up. I was cajoled and eventually and very reluctantly put my hand up. I was never any good at football, and never learnt any rules when I was a lad. But that didn't matter. While Martin organized the club, obtained sponsorship and got the lads a kit. I was off to Ref School.

I think most referees can remember attending their course. For those who cannot, mine was a condensed course, consisting of two full Saturdays. I was very nervous when I turned up. There were tons of 14 year olds, some 17/18 year olds, a couple of managers and 2 women. The referee coaches introduced themselves and then started having an argument between themselves. Another coach appeared, donned in referees attire. He blew his whistle. The two coaches carried on arguing and the referee slowly calmed them down. He then turned to us and asked each of us to write a report of what just happen. Homework already and only 2 minutes into the course. The rest of the day covered the 17 laws.

I was lucky to work with Mike Bull, a Premiership Assistant Referee, and asked for his opinion when writing reports. His simple advice was to be concise, accurate and cover the salient points. Over the years he has been a great mentor.

The second Saturday, we read out our reports. It was amazing to find out how many attendees believed that they had heard the two coaches swear. The rest of the morning dealt with questions various people had, then off to lunch. On our return, it our horror, we had our exam. Gruelling and difficult but the old examiners were great. So with a pass mark of 97% I had done it. As I walked out I was asked if I wanted to buy a new referee shirt. I chose short sleeve and asked for the county badge.

Diary of a New Referee

So there I stood, shirt in hand qualified, proud as punch. I had done it!

Diary of a New Referee

My First Match.

I turned up at Pound Lane in Epsom for my first match against Harding Pumas. My little 6 year boy was in goal, decked out in his new white Stoneleigh Athletic jersey, gloves and his Chelsea cap. The rest of the team were raring to go. Mums and Dads cheering on their special little one. There I stood nervous as anything decked out in my shiny new black kit. Socks pulled up, whistle in my left hand, watch on my left arm and notebook in my right pocket. I looked around and no one was looking at me. I had been nervous for nothing. All eyes were on the lads. I blew my whistle, and the lads kicked off.

Within minutes of the starting I blew up for the first time, desperate the make my first decision the correct one. 'Off side I shouted', indicating with my arm along the line. Coach Martin ran on to the pitch and had a quite word with me. 'We don't have offside in youth 7 aside football', he explained. So in my very first match, my very first decision was wrong!

I restarted the game with a drop ball. At least I got that decision right.

Stoneleigh Athletic won the match 4 - 2.

Child Abuse.

We skip forward. Martin had decided that the Pound Lane had too many ditches and the pitch not to his players liking. This may been seen as arrogant from outsiders, but the lads had been taught passing the ball around the park and keeping the wingers wide. Most other sides just follow the ball, and if you had a hoop, you could cover most players. Martin had drilled his players to stay wide and let the ball do the work. This strategy had worked the previous season and secured the lads Premier status, finishing 3rd in the league. A fantastic achievement in their first season.

Martin had secured a new pitch at New Malden's Kings College. He informed Stoneleigh Athletic, who suggested the ground should for their older teams. In the end Martin broke away from Stoneleigh and formed his own club with just one team.

Now at Kings College with a new name; Kings played on a billiard green of a pitch. Their passing improved and so did their league rankings.

In December, Kings played Rosetta Giants at home. This was going to be a thriller of a game. Rosetta Giants were the team to beat. They were league champions the previous season and won a bucket load of trophies during the summer.

The game started well enough, with both sides pressing. Reminiscent of two fencers in combat, thrust and parry. The second half began in the same vein, with no goals scored so far. Kings were playing above themselves. Rosetta Giants were getting frustrated. No more so than the Rosetta Coach. He called 'ref, substitute'. When the ball had gone out for a Rosetta Throw.

Now there is nothing in the LOTG that states substitutes have to be made if a coach calls for one, nor if the player does not want to come off, the referee cannot force him. So what happen next took me by surprise. Let's not forget that this was the beginning of my second season, with only a dozen games under my belt.

As the player started to walk towards the touchline, the coach called out to his player. 'Anup! Stop and look around. Every other player is working hard. You're not! You're lazy. You need to work

Diary of a New Referee

harder'. The lad was crying, and very upset. The coach then said 'I've changed my mind ref, play on.'

I approached the Rosetta Coach, explaining that he shouldn't talk to his players. His responded that he didn't care what I said, and didn't respect me as a referee. I asked him to be quiet, but he carried on, adding. 'I don't respect you, and I'll say it again, that's 3 times I don't respect you.' Not wanting to get into a verbal melee in the presence of these young players, I restarted the match. Some may say that I handled this badly, but with only a dozen games under my belt, and never experienced this level of abuse before, I felt I could deal with this off the pitch. The FA had brought in The Respect campaign, which I believed in it.

So the game ended with Rosetta Giants winning 3 - 0. All I had to do was report the 'incident' to the league. The coach would get his comeuppance and everything would be fine. Wrong. I did report the Rosetta coach for Child abuse and dissent, nothing appeared to happen

The league said I should have dealt with it on the pitch. This is not right. New referees want assistance and guidance and more importantly support. What I received was none of this. However I had an ace up my sleeve.

During that year I came across a local radio show called Surrey Soccer, hosted by an incredible charismatic man Mike Smith. He was passionate and talked about all aspects of grassroots football. One of his guests however was none other than Tim Lawrence, Referee Development Office for the County FA. I mentioned the abuse I and the young lad received, and was asked to send in details. Tim responded very quickly indeed. He said he would look into the allegations about the lad at his level, and provided me with detailed steps to deal with future occurrences.

If the level of abuse if not offensive but distracting then use the ask, tell, eject method.

• **ASK**, the coach or person to keep his comments to himself.

- **TELL**, you already asked him to be quiet, now you are telling him. If he carries on he will have to leave.

- **EJECT**. you've asked and told him, he now has to leave. Tell him the game will not restart until he leaves. If he fails to leave, then abandon the game and inform the league.

If the level of abuse is offensive, just ask him to leave. Tell him the game will not restart until he leaves. If he fails to leave, then abandon the game and inform the league.

While I have not ejected any coaching staff, I have used the **Ask**, **Tell**, **Eject** method successfully and we will come to this later.

Diary of a New Referee

Referee Abuse.

Now at grassroots level, for ten years and below, it is frowned upon by many leagues to caution players let alone send them off from the field of play. Referees know this, parents know this and unfortunately so do some kids.

So in November, Kings took on Winterton Juniors. The game was feisty and fraught. While Kings attacked, Winterton Juniors managed to scramble the ball away and into touch. However, on one occasion a young Winterton Juniors took offense to a Kings challenge where the ball went off for a Winterton throw.

Deep in Winterton's half, just right of the penalty area, both players went for the ball. Both kicked the ball, and the ball went out of play. I indicated a throw for Winterton Juniors. Unfortunately the Winterton player stated shouting, **'He kicked me Ref! What are you going to do about it? I want a free kick!'** I replied **'No, you have a throw, play on'**. The lad then started his rant... 'He **kicked me... kicked me.... you cheater....'** I looked at the dad who had come on the pitch, very apologetic. I held my tongue, backing away..

Should have cautioned this lad for dissent? He was throwing his toys out of his pram making quite a spectacle. His dad was very embarrassed, trying to grab his son and asking his to quiet down. While all the time this lad continued his barrage. '**You cheater, he kicked me, you cheater....'** The only way to deal with this is to caution the lad, otherwise he will never learn. But unfortunately at this level, the referee hands are tied. We can only administer cards for hitting and spitting etc, but most referees have a quiet word with the managers first. The words 'Take him off before I do', always seem to work wonders.

Diary of a New Referee

Corner Blow.

In every game as a new referee, mistakes are bound to happen. We are only human. The referee sees the game from one angle in real time. Around the pitch dozens of spectators and parents who see the game through rose tinted glasses. The referee may be playing advantage, or just about to blow for a foul, and you get a comment thrown from the touch line. These you generally ignore, and over the years you develop thick skin to deal with comment and their opinion. And don't forget, it is in the opinion of the referee that counts. However you must be aware when to blow the whistle and when not to blow the whistle.

I had always thought from the mountains of helping guides to blow when the game restarts, such as restart of the game and free kicks. However I added corners to this list as to switch on the players after the ball has gone out of play. How wrong was I.

In November, Kings were playing Bryne at Kings College. During the feisty game, with Kings leading 1-0, Kings won a corner. As with most corners, the ball had been kicked a fair way away, and the lad had run after it. He positioned the ball and waited. With all corners the ref usually focuses on the players in the penalty area, looking for pushing and holding etc. while I was still looking at the lads in the penalty area, I was conscience the ball hadn't been kicked so I blew my whistle. Unbeknown to me, the kicker was just running up to the ball as I blew. He kicked the ball and all the Kings players stopped. I shouted '**play on**'. My second mistake. Bryne received the ball, kicking it up the pitch. The Kings players were like rabbits in headlights, just standing there. Slowly they began to recover, but it was too late. Bryne had three players attacking with two to beat. Needless to say they scored.

The Kings coach wasn't very happy. I reffed the game fairly and honestly. My only mistake was not knowing the LOTG [Laws of the Game]. This was a wakeup call for me.

Back to School.

When one makes a complete hash of a game, it stays with you and eats away at you. I heard this before but never believed that it would affect me this bad. It was a simple mistake, but it affected the result and I felt I had let down football. So I hit the books looking for an insight to the different aspects of football that are not covered by the LOTG. Yes the interpretation of the LOTG helped, but I was looking for something more.

Scanning the internet I came across a public domain PDF by Julian Carosi. While this covered the LOTG, there were pages dedicated to questions and answers for each law. This was it. I started to get back into the boots of a referee. I was no longer alone. Finally after 588 pages I felt I was ready to vent my knowledge.

I have already mentioned Mike Smith's Surrey Soccer with Tim Lawrence, Referee Development Office for the County FA. On this show Mike started a section called 'Beat the Ref', where questions were asked, and listeners emailed in their answers.

Such as, which of the following is mandatory on the field of play.

1.   Goal nets.
2.   Corner flags.
3.   Assistant Referees.

I was hooked, but I wanted more. And in my pursuit to gain more knowledge I came across various podcasts. Chapper's Premier League where Graham Poll entertained everyone with his humour, and the US Soccer podcast. This was totally aimed at referees, providing insights from actual games coupled with their website and video clips. All public domain. You could actually see the foul, or offside offense. Now while these were all US games, I still learnt a lot from our US colleagues.

Man-management is something you are not taught. It is learnt during your career, but listening to Brian Hall, Manager of Referee Assessment and Training, and watching those video clips, the pieces of the jigsaw began to fall into place and I began to see the bigger picture. Yes I was still fussy around the edges, but I had confidence, and the finer aspects of the LOTG I now

Diary of a New Referee

understood. Such as when to flag for offside. Brian suggested the **wait-and-see** approach. Wait for the player, who is in a off-side position, to interfere with play or an opponent before flagging. It was these little snippet that gave me my new found confidence.

Now with my new found knowledge, I just needed to put it into practice.

Two-Touch Keeper.

One morning in March, during a great game between Greytown and Kings at New Malden. The Greytown keeper collected the ball from a slack shot. The King's player ran out of the penalty area ready for the next phase. The Greytown keeper, seeing that he had plenty of space started walking towards the edge of his penalty area. Still within his area he dropped the ball to the ground and tapped it forward. Quick-witted Archie, the King's striker, ran towards the Greytown keeper. I moved away from the expected landing zone and towards the penalty area. The Greytown keeper seeing this threat immediately picked the ball up again, and I blew my whistle; indirect free-kick.

With youth football, all free kicks are direct. Kings had a free kick on the edge of the penalty area. Archie placed the ball on the ground and the ball ended in the back of the net. The game ended 5-2.

After Premiership games, coaches are not allowed to talk to referees for an additional 30 minutes. This allows coaches to calm down and think about incidents. However when reffing at grassroots level, we never seem to have this luxury. So on this occasion, within minutes of the final whistle the Greytown coach found me. I knew want he wanted to discuss before he started talking. He was a tad upset, **'How do you expect the kids to know all the rules? You should have let our keeper pick the ball up!'**. Using my new man-management I explained that I had to play to the laws. I couldn't change the law for goal kicks, corners etc. additionally the keeper had now learnt his lesson and that he wouldn't do it again.

Referees have a duty to uphold the LOTG. If the situation expects a caution or red card then you must issue the caution or red card. So if you have a DOGSO [Deny an obvious goal scoring opportunity] , then as a referee you must issue a red card. If you fail to produce what is expected, then you are will lose respect of the players, the coaching staff and the crowd. You would have failed the game. So on your next big decision, make sure you give what is expected, just as long as you make a fair and honest decision. And don't forget the decisions you make on the field of play are in your opinion of the referee.

Diary of a New Referee

Tone is Important.

Player man-management can always be difficult. You need to create your own style over many games, but this is one aspect of the game that you need to learn by yourself. Some say to become the best you need to emulate the best. Pierluigi Collina, the bald Italian, was probably the best referee in the world and he ensures that he knew each players names and their positions. How they would react if they were losing, or which players might get involved in incidents behind his back. He was masterful.

I am not saying that you need to know every player's name. However, you can learn some. The skilful players, the crunching tacklers and those less adept. I also look out for those players who get annoyed quickly as these are usually the ones that cause you trouble in tackles.

Now that you know some players, you need to start talking to them. Not continuous banter for the whole game, but provide praise when due, or conversely **'keep the arm down in the next challenge'**. I found out that if I explained why I had given a foul, truly explained then I had better man-management over the players. I sometimes talked through the captains if I felt Joe or Jamie were getting too spirited. However, it is the tone that truly sells it.

I remember one game when one player had made a number of clumsy challenges. His last challenge was over the ball and unfortunately struck the defenders leg. The injured lad was in agony and the attacker was standing over him. I anticipated the challenge, I was on the scene within 5 strides. I was exacerbated by the challenge and told the attacker to 'Go Away!' My tone sharp and harsh. I turned and started to calm down the physio, who was screaming. When I turned back the attacker was nowhere to be seen. Looking around I found him on the touch line, crying. The 10 year old lad knew what he has done was wrong and had believed I had sent him off. I hadn't.

So while you have all the man-management skills, it can all be undermined by using the wrong tone. You need to be calm in these situations, controlled and not let your emotions run away. From that moment on, I always ask myself how would Pierluigi Collina handle the situation. He's firm, confident and always in

Diary of a New Referee

control of his emotions. I have used this technique in several games after this incident and it does work.

Judo Throw.

Kings played away at Bryne. A crisp autumnal morning, the sun shining over the treetops. A really splendid start to the day. And this was one game I was just a spectator. I included this as it shows what can happen at games where there isn't a qualified referee, and just a dad in the middle. Now I don't mind dads reffing, but they must know the LOTG and not keep referring to the bench for every decision. Unfortunately on this occasion the dad thought he was doing the right thing, he may have been cajoled into the middle.

The ball was expertly passed from midfield and Tyler collected it in mid-stride down the right wing. Using his skills he stepped over and passed the first defender. A second player ran alongside Tyler, interlinking arms vying for the ball. He then lunged for the ball, unceremoniously sticking his backside into Tyler's side and using his arm, threw him to the ground. The challenge was unnecessary, cynical, deliberate and malicious.

Unfortunately the referee's hands have been tied by the local league ruling. Both yellow and red cards have been discouraged at this age group. I spoke to both sides after the game and was taken aback by their bipolar comments:

"What? There nothing wrong with that challenge. My lad shielded the ball and the other guy fell over. In a senior game that wouldn't even be a free kick."

And the other coach's comments.

"If one my lads did that he'd be off straight away. I will not tolerate it."

The referee dad, looked over at the Bryne's bench as if for guidance. He blew his whistle and wordlessly restarted with a free kick.

Should cards be issued at this level or should they be discouraged? Without discipline for these dangerous, callous challenges, how will the kids ever learn. It has been widely published that the FA will not tolerate dangerous tackles, nor should grass root football.

Diary of a New Referee

Playing Advantage.

Later that season, Kings were playing at home against Melmoth. It was a tight game and Kings were pressing for a second goal, however Melmoth countered beating the defence who were quite high up the pitch. It was Melmoth striker against keeper. The striker ran in to the penalty area on the right, being right-footed, in line with the 6 yard line. The keeper came out quickly and slid towards the striker.

The LOTG game state that a keeper may make contact with another player as long as s/he makes contact with the ball first. This doesn't mean that the keeper can touch the ball, then five minutes later make contact with an opposing player. It means a split second later. However you need to take into account the keepers intent. Was he looking at the ball or player? How fast was he travelling? Was it reckless?

So when the keeper came out quickly towards the striker I made sure that I was at the penalty area to sell the decision, whatever the outcome. The keeper on his left side slid towards the feet of the striker, however the striker had deft feet and jinked towards his right, away from goal. Then lifted the ball over the keeper. Well that is what he intended to do. As the player jinked right the keeper collided with the strikers left leg with his shins. His momentum carried the keepers arms towards the ball, making contact. This lifted the ball upwards which then hit the strikers head. The ball then proceeded to travel towards goal.

So it going to be a goal then. I didn't need to give a penalty nor caution. I had played advantage and it panned out. No. It didn't. A defender had ran back and seeing the tackle with the ball heading towards goal had strained every sinew to get to the ball before it crossed the line. With one final lunge the defender had managed to clear the ball. It happened so fast, about 2 seconds had elapsed. I had played advantage and it hadn't worked. So I pointed to the penalty mark. The keeper stood up and argued that he had got the ball first. While he may be my son, I made an honest decision and in my opinion a correct one. He had hit the striker before the ball. I was close to the incident and could still sell the decision.

Diary of a New Referee

What I had done wrong however was to give advantage. The ball was going towards goal and if it had gone in I wouldn't need to have pointed to the penalty mark. I wouldn't have need to caution the keeper. At the point of impact the striker was heading away from goal, so I couldn't give a red card because it wasn't an obvious goal scoring opportunity.

Discussing this point with many referees over the years has provided two schools of thought. But I finally agreed that I should only give advantage for a split-second, and if there is no obvious advantage. Such as an instant goal, then give a penalty. Do not wait too long before blowing the whistle as I did. I was lucky. My proximity to play was excellent, my position was excellent. I just waited slightly too long. I was wrong. I awarded a penalty and cautioned the keeper.

Diary of a New Referee

Penalty Laws.

Penalty kicks and Kicks from the Penalty Mark are two separate events. One happens during the game, the other is at the end of the game to decide a winner, such as cup games.

While basic, I thought I would just recap some of the basic procedures and some of the laws that I needed during my games.

Penalty Kick.

- The referee managers the players and the kicker, and monitors infringement. But not the keeper.
- Stands between the penalty mark and the penalty area, but just outside the line between the 6 yard and the penalty arc. This way he can see the kicker and other players.
- Confirms AR signals for a goal scored or infringement.

Assistant Referee.

- Stands on the intersection of the penalty area and the goal line.
- Monitors infringement of the keeper.
- Signals if a goal was correctly scored.
- Returns quickly to the touchline is the ball remains in play.

The keeper cannot move forward before the kick has been taken. Players not involved with the taking of the penalty cannot enter the penalty area until the ball has moved forward.

Kicks from the penalty mark phase begins immediately after the whistle signals the end of regulation play, including any additional time. Only players who were on the field of play at the end of regulation time can be involved.

When a team finishes the match with a greater number of players than their opponents, they shall reduce their numbers to equate with that of their opponents and inform the referee the name and number of the player excluded.

A keeper who is injured while kicks are being taken from the penalty mark and is unable to continue may be replaced with a named substitute provided that team has not used the maximum number of substitutes.

A player other than the keeper who is injured may not be substituted during the taking of kicks from the penalty mark.

An eligible player may change places with the keeper at any time as long as the referee is notified.

If a keeper is sent off during kicks from the penalty mark, he shall be replaced by a player who finished the match.

If a player is sent off during kicks from the penalty mark and the team has one player less, the referee should not reduce the number of players taking kicks for the other team. An equal number of players from each team is required only at the start of the taking of kicks from the penalty mark.

Diary of a New Referee

A Game of Two Referees.

Later that year, I attended an away game between Winterton and Kings where the referee had not turned up. It was late Saturday afternoon and the light was fading but the lads wanted to play. They didn't want to travel all that way only to have the game cancelled. The away manager knew me and had seen me referee many times and asked if I could ref his game. As I had a spare referee kit in my car I agreed.

The game started without incident although 10 minutes late. I gave a penalty to the home team within 10 minutes of blowing the whistle as two defenders sandwiched the striker in the penalty area.

The game continued, and the home team scored another game. Then with five minutes left in the first half the away team started to fight back. Challenges that were half-hearted earlier became full blooded tackles. Using man-management skills I defused the situations. Either through the captain or directly at the player. The game was bubbling and neither the game nor player needed a card. I was on top of the situation, and talking to the players. I blew up for half time with the score 2-1.

During the halftime interlude I was informed by the home coach, that the allotted referee had finally turned up, and that he wanted the allotted referee to finish out the game. I was only helping out, so I obliged. I walked up to the young 18 year old referee, and handed over my score sheet. I attempted to inform him who to look out for and those who I had previously warned. With what smelled like alcohol on his breathe he said he didn't care. Turned his back and walked away.

The second half became feistier and feistier, challenges went in, elbows went in, and the referee just ignored them.

The game finally ended 2-2, and the away side started rounding on me. Why I had stopped reffing?

I later found out that I should have continued reffing the game. I had been told that if you start the game as a referee you must finish as a referee. The only exception is if you become injured and cannot continue. During my pre match discussions with assistant referees now, I always ensure that they know who will be taking over from me if I am injured.

Diary of a New Referee

Handball Ref!

How many times have you heard the call from players, 'Hand ball ref!' I've lost count. In my pre game discussions with the players I tell them to play to the whistle, and if I believe the handball is deliberate I will give it.

The LOTG state that handball must be deliberate. In other words the action must be a premeditated action, to move ones arm into the path of the ball. This includes moving the arm or shoulder towards the ball. Additionally the arm cannot be in an unnatural position, for example above a players head.

However, if a striker kicks the ball towards goal and the defender is only yards away and he does have time to react and move his arm away. He cannot be penalized. If on the other hand the striker has 20 yards away, and the defender seeing the ball had time to move his hands away, but decided to leave it in the path of the ball. Then this would be handball.

I use the following rule to decide it the handball was deliberate:

- Involuntary, where your hands move by instinct to protect the body.

- Reactionary, where you knowingly react to the fight of the ball.

If the Ref's whistle blows, players stop. Otherwise play continues.

During the taking of a ceremonial free kick, I ensure that the defenders in the wall are aware that if they move their arms after the ball is kicked and it hits their arms, I will award a free kick or penalty. I only have to mention this once or twice during the game and it serves me well.

What becomes contentious is when a player puts his arms up because he believes he was fouled, and the ball lands on his outstretched arm. Even if the player is unaware of the ball or not even facing the ball, is this deliberate?

Diary of a New Referee

This happened during the Norwich Blackburn game on September 30th, 2011 where Steven N'zonzi, defending deep in his penalty area challenging for the ball, was sandwiched by two Norwich attacking players. N'zonzi believed he should be awarded a free kick and raised his arms claiming a free kick to the ref. Unfortunately the ball was in the air at the time N'zonzi claimed for a free kick. The ball landed on N'zonzi left outstretched arm. Anthony Taylor, the referee, awarded a penalty.

Was it a penalty? The arms were in an unnatural position and maybe Anthony believed N'zonzi just had his arms up deliberately which constitutes a handball.

Handball has to be deliberate. It is all about getting in to the mind of the player, did he mean to put his hand in the way of the ball. Putting your hands up is a deliberate act. Doing it in front of goal preventing an obvious a goal scoring opportunity is a dismissible offense.

Diary of a New Referee

Studs.

In one of the last games for Kings in the season they played Bryne at New Malden. The league table was close. Bryne needed to win this game and their next to win the league. Kings just needed a draw. This was billed as the local derby, and drew lots of spectators. Both teams had played each other earlier that season and the game finished 3-1 Bryne.

As a referee I try and understand the history of the sides playing, what were the issues when the sides met earlier. So when I turned up for the match, I knew it was going to be a feisty hard game to control.

During the pre match talk, I instructed the players and coaches to control their tackling. I didn't want any over-the-ball lunges, nor any two-footed tackles. I instructed the players to keep their arms down when jumping for the ball. I didn't want any broken legs nor elbows to the head at this late stage of the season.

They started okay, with Kings kicking off, the ball was passed back to the left back. Bryne had been hounding the Kings players forcing the ball back. So with a poor ball back to the King's left back, the Bryne striker quickened his pace. I had been on the left of the pitch, but quickly dropped back.

The first 10 minutes are important, the referee needs to be strict and it sets out his intentions for the game. If you let harsh tackles go in the first 10 minutes, the players will take this as you are happy, and they will continue. By being forceful and close to play you will be able control the game with good man management.

So when the ball was passed back poorly to the Kings left back, the Bryne striker sprinted and jumped for the ball. His left foot was sidewards, high and over the ball. His right foot landed on the ball. This is one of those tackles that is cringing to watch. The Kings player did see the striker coming in, but late, and managed to jump up. However contact was made. Only 10 seconds had elapsed. The Kings manager went ballistic, shouting at the Bryne manager, who in turn argued that his lad had got the ball.

Diary of a New Referee

This is when you need to draw on the man-management skills, not only for the striker but for the managers. Firstly I had to calm down the Kings coach, who was on the pitch dealing with the left back shouting at the Bryne player and coach. Secondly I had to deal with the Bryne striker. Thirdly, I had to deal with the Bryne manager, explaining that he needs to calm his players down. You need to be forceful but not rude, direct, and to the point. It has to be a one-way conversation, without backchat. Yes this should have been a red card and the player should have not been allowed to stay on the field of play to repeat his actions and possibly break an opponent's leg.

However, this issuing of cards are frowned upon at this level of football by the officiating league. You will need to check with your league and act accordingly on the field of play.

After this exchange, they game calmed down and resulted in Kings winning 3-0

Effing C.

The morning started quite well after arriving at the Durban ground. The sun was shining with no sign of any wind. I was going to be one of the assistant referees so I sought out the referee for the game against Kings. I found this chap all decked out in black standing in the centre circle. As I walked up to I thought to myself that he looked incredibly small. He was 14 and had only recently passed.

He welcomed me and then asked a strange question. **'How do I send off a parent?'** The alarms bells immediately ran in my head. Did he know something that I did not? Were these omens for the game? Nonetheless, I explained that he should use the Ask, Tell and Eject method as we previously covered in this diary.

- **ASK**, the coach or person to be keep his comments to himself.

- **TELL**, you already asked him to be quiet, now you are telling him. If he carries on you will ask him to leave.

- **EJECT**. you've asked and told him, now it time to ask him to leave. Tell him the game will not restart until he leaves. If he fails to leave, then abandon the game and inform the league.

The young lad asked me if he needed to eject any parent would I help. 'Of course I would', I replied.

The game kicked off, and in the first half I side-stepped up and down the line providing assistance to the referee with throw and the odd offside. He was doing an admiral job.

But it was in the second half that things began to happen. As with all grassroots games the assistant referee who runs the line parents side is always open to abuse. In my case however I was aware of a parent tracking my runs. On one occasion where the Durban striker made a magnificent run, the Kings back line stepped up just as the ball was kicked.

Diary of a New Referee

Offside. The firsts words started to inch towards my ears. The second occasion was where the Durban striker was standing in an offside position, waiting for the ball near my touchline. The ball was kicked up and towards him. Two Kings defenders on the far side started to run back towards goal. By the time the Durban striker received the ball the Kings players had ran back, making the striker onside. I raised my flag when the Durban striker touched the ball. A torrid of abuse erupted behind me. 'You effing cheat, you effing cheat' I turned and asked him to be quiet. But he continued to shout abuse. I then told him to be quite otherwise he would be ejected. The enraged parent continued his ranting.

At this point I walked on to the pitch making distance between the spectator and myself. While walking on the pitch I indicated to the referee that the spectator needed to be removed. Just like we had discussed earlier. However, this 14 year old indicated that I should be the one to do the ejection. I turned and walked toward the Durban manager asking him to eject the parent. The parent then shouted further abuse, 'you f@cking c€nt, you talking to me!' I then explained to the manager, that the game may be abandoned and/or the club fined if the parent continued. I then backed away towards the pitch. The manager was brilliant. He dealt with the matter, removing the spectator from the ground.

While these sideline antics were going ahead, the referee had cautioned the player I had flagged for being offside. As he had walked past the referee, he had sworn while facing the referee. The game continued without further incident.

At the end of the game, the referee was physically shaken. I walked over to him and asked if he was okay. He said yes, but I knew there was something wrong. I stayed in the centre circle while the young referee walked away. Five minutes later he came back scared and asked tentatively if I would help him get his match fee. I walked bodyguard style over to the Durban manager and the referee got paid. I found it outrageous that any referee should feel scared on the pitch let alone a 14 year old lad. How intimidated do you think the poor lad would have felt if I hadn't been there especially as he was there for the whole day.

Diary of a New Referee

After getting his money he disappeared for 10 minutes, and I walked to the touch line to collect my bag and have a drink of water. The lad was back and this time asking if I knew who the manager was for the next game as he didn't want to ref anymore that day. We found the manager of the next game and had a long chat with him, explaining what a torrid time he had. The manager was brilliant and together we convinced the referee to stay to officiate the game.

I reported the incident to the league, so did the young referee. I later found out that he had two blinding games that day. Well done.

The mouthy spectator still watches Durban games, and he hasn't changed. I hear he was just as obnoxious at a recent Bryne cup game.

As Ray Winston says, coaches should encourage, parents should keep their mouths shut.

Assistant Referee.

Assistant Referees have a job to assist the referee in his or her job. It is not their place to embarrass the referee or take over the game. They are a team, with the referee is in charge.

During pre-game talks, the referee should cover the duties of the assistant referee, which some include;

- Indicate when the ball goes out for a throw or corner.
- Offsides, using the wait and see approach.
- Where to stand during corner, and to indicate if the ball crosses the line.
- Where to stand during penalties.
- Where to stand and look for during goal kicks.
- Where to stand and look for during melees.
- Keep eye contact with the referee.
- Mass confrontation.

So there I was at a Bryne away game, running the line, I ensured that I followed the referees instructions. Arm up for throws. As an assistant referee your need to be 100 percent certain with your decisions. If you are not sure, look at the referee who may give you a little signal with his hands. On those occasions where the referee does not know, he will look towards you as the assistant. If neither of you know whose throw it is, the referee will generally go with the defending team. However this is not your decision, it is the referees. As I mentioned before, you have to be 100 percent of your decisions. By doing this, you are not only helping your referee, but also helping your credibility for when you make those crucial off side decisions.

When the ball clearly came off a Bryne head for a throw I raised my flag and indicated up field for a Kings throw. I was looking at the referee for any sign prior to flagging, as he would walk in the direction of the throw ready for the next phase of play. However he looked at me and shrugged his shoulders. I stood firm and the referee followed my lead. The Bryne bench reacted badly, shouting down the line at me that their player hadn't touched the ball. In the incidents you have to be strong and not change your mind. If the referee wants to talk to you, then he will do so. On this occasion he went with my lead.

Diary of a New Referee

From the throw-in, the Kings passed the ball ten times before their strike on goal, beating the keeper to his left. The Bryne bench remonstrated, saying my decision had cost them a goal. I have learnt not to get involved in arguments with players nor coaches after the match. In the premiership coaches and managers cannot talk to the referee for 30 minute, as this gives them a cooling down period. So after every game I wonder off to the changing room, leaving the coaches to talk to his players and instruct any warm down practices.

High Foot.

Early Autumn, Kings were away to Sheffield Beach and yet another autumnal morning. The designated referee had not turned up. Within 10 minutes of kick off the call went out to get a replacement. With minutes to kick off, the replacement referee walked on to the pitch. After a quick pre match chat, I took up position on the line.

Sheffield Beach had played Kings before. This should have alerted the Kings that it would be a tough game but it was to be a day when Kings were very slow out of the blocks, and simply never caught up against a strong newly promoted team keen to make their mark.

Sheffield Beach played one two from a throw in down in the left corner and a shot from the Sheffield striker was fisted clear by the keeper. With Sheffield lofting the ball over the top, the Kings keeper was twice fast off his line to deny the approaching forwards but on the third occasion everything went wrong.

With the Kings defensive line high up the pitch and the Sheffield striker hovering on the half way line. The Sheffield midfielder hoofed the ball up field over the Kings high line.

The referee was positioned in the centre circle. The Sheffield striker pounced, beating the offside trap and sprinted down my wing. The ball bounced around the 30 yard mark heading for the penalty area in line with the penalty area parallel line. The referee moved up the pitch following play, but behind the players. The Kings keeper ran out as he had done previously, to meet the ball. However the ball bounced again outside the penalty area. It was keeper versus striker. The ball went up. The striker jumped for the ball as it came down. The keeper jumped for the ball. The striker went to header the ball over the keeper. The keeper went to clear the ball with his.....err, foot. The striker received a size 9 to his chest and crumpled to the ground.

I waved my flag and indicated yellow card. However the referee waved me off. But don't forget, assistance referees are there for one reason. To assist the referee. Not to run on to the field of play and tell him he is wrong. So I took up position in readiness for the free kick.

Diary of a New Referee

The referee walked over to the Kings keeper, calling him by name and walked with him towards his goal. He told the keeper he had done nothing wrong, and not to be upset. The referee then went back to the Sheffield player, who had his shirt raised by the physio who were dealing with the boot mark to the chest, and indicated a free kick.

A great free kick, over the wall, and towards the near post. The keeper blocked the shot but couldn't hold on to the ball. The Sheffield striker pounced and knocked it in on the rebound.

At half time I wondered over to the referee who had taken up position on the far touch line. He was talking to the keeper's dad. As I got within earshot, he was saying that he had enjoyed the dinner party they had the night before. Was this why the keeper was not cautioned?

When you walk on to the field of play as a referee you must leave your friendship at the door. Certain actions on the pitch have expectations on the referee, such as:

- Denial of an obvious goal scoring opportunity.
- Dangerous play.
- Spitting.
- Dissent.

Whenever these happen you have a obligation to deal with it. If you fail to react as expected then you lose your credibility on the pitch, the players will then start to take matters into their own hands and the game quickly becomes a farce.

I urge you to leave all friendship etc when you walk on to the pitch, if you cannot, don't become a referee nor assistant referee.

Jack the Biscuit

We have all seen the Ray Winston videos dealing with Respect, but how often do we see it practiced on the pitch. During my short career so far, I have only experienced it once, and we discussed that in an earlier chapter. However later that year, I had the unfortunate task of dealing with it.

Glencoe were against Kosi Bay down at the Rosetta ground for a 9:30 kick off. It was dry, not much wind, but dew had been sprinkled over the pitch. The game started brightly for Glencoe, with Kosi Bay going down a goal within the opening minutes. Then I heard it, parents shouting at Kosi Bay. Chase the ball, do this, get involved. A constant barrage of instructions from the spectator side.

Most matches, if not all, have crowds shouting. Just look at the terraces of any given match day. However with youth football it has to be constructive.

During the game, not only do I encourage the players; great tackle etc I also remind them to keep elbows down in tackles and explain why a freekick was awarded. I am continuously looking around the pitch, but when I see a player crying you need to find out why.

Jerome, was having a marvellous game. Chasing ball, making space and delivering some great passes. Two or more were a little wayward, but he chased back. Unfortunately he visibly recoiled and his head lowered, whenever this single spectator started shouting. I asked him if he was okay, thinking he had been hurt in a tackle or something. But no, he was upset because of the abuse he was getting from the touch line. While to ball was out for a goal kick I asked him if he was okay and whether we wanted me to deal with the shouting. He smiled. So with only seconds before half time, I waited for the kick and blew.

During the half time break I called the Kosi Bay Manager over and explained my concerns. I asked him politely to have a word with the spectator. To the manager's credit, he talked to Jerome's mother.

Jerome's demeanour changed in the second half, his game was totally different. The slack passes in the first half had gone, and he showed some great skills to get into Glencoe's penalty area to score.

As referees we all have a responsibility to protect the rising stars of tomorrow. I did my part today and that was reflected in a changed player. I hope the coach has learned something today. As Ray Winton says in his Respect videos, we need to deal with Jack the Biscuit otherwise we won't have a game.

The Final Whistle

I originally believed the blowing of the final whistle was always regimental. When time is up, no matter where the ball is, time is up and the referee blows for full time. However I started to challenge this belief.

If the attacking blue team were fouled within seconds of the final whistle, should they be allowed to complete their attack. Failure to allow the natural attack to flow just encourages the defending team to foul more often in the closing minutes. And this is not what you want as a referee. You are tired, the players are more so. So it would be prudent to allow the attacking side to complete their attack.

The world renowned public domain Referees World Podcast hosted by Darren Cullum and PGMO Assessor Richard Melinn raise some good points.

What would you do if there was only 30 seconds on the watch left to play.

Example 1.
Score line is 3-0 it doesn't matter whose winning. The losing side have been beaten soundly, you may have cautioned or sent off players. Don't prolong the experience. Does it matter that you stop play 10 seconds early - ideally when the ball is in defence or midfield.

Example 2.
Score line is 0-0, it is a cup match, and it looks like there will be extra time. Can you get a result without being controversial?

How long does it take for play to move from defence to attack 10-15 seconds? Let the attack finish, so what if you played slightly over. If a goal was scored , restart from the centre circle and then blow final whistle. It could be the best cup match ever and decided decisively without incident.

Example 3.
Tight league match score line 1-0 and losing team is pressing for equalizer. Using game management and empathy allow 10-

15secs. Referee is sole discretion of time played or extended time for stoppages.

Consider the following when reading the above examples:

- Does / did the referee stop the watch every time the ball is out of play? **No**

- Discretion and management of time is only the referee's decision not spectators, players or the assessor.

- However, if you're refereeing on the TV that's a different issue because they will have the clock ticking down so precise timing is standard expectation .

10 Point plan to become a successful Referee.

The following ten point plan is a guide to help you become a successful referee.

> Believe in yourself. This will help your confidence on and off the field of play.

> Think positive, a mindset for success. Go out on the field of play and believe in yourself using a positive mindset. Develop your skills

> Transfer the knowledge off the pitch onto the field of play. Practice, practice, practice before you go on the field of play. What will you say to players after a foul, what hand signals are you going to use.

> Solicit feedback on your performance, not just from assessors, or coaches, but from players too.

> Control the controllable. You know the LOTG, use your skills on the field of play. If you see it deal with it.

> Be smart, not just in your appearance, but be smart on the field of play. Are you going to wait for comment at a free kick or are you going to carry on with the game.

> Be tough at the right time. If you see denial of an obvious goal scoring opportunity, then don't disappoint. If you take your eye off the ball and give a yellow for a denial, then your credibility goes straight out the window.

> Engage your senses. Don't lose your concentration especially in the last quarter of the game. Keep your focus and try to relax.

> Prepare, prepare, prepare every area of your referee performance. How do you look when you give a signal. Do you know? Practice in the mirror.

> Enjoy the moment, and enjoy refereeing.

Diary of a New Referee

Hooked.

During this diary I have shared a number of incidents where I made a few mistakes. Most referees do, we are only human. But I had noticed that my game had improved dramatically and received positive comments. So nearing year end I was to be the referee for the local derby; Kings against Bryne.

You may have noticed in this diary, there has always been issues between these two teams. So it wasn't surprising that I was a little nervous. But then nervousness is a good thing as it heightens your senses. If used correctly it can make a good performance, a great performance.

I arrived at the New Malden ground at 9am, about 90 minutes before kickoff, got changed and ran out to the pitch. New Malden has 14 pitches, so the run out was part of my warm up routine. I usually do a couple of circuits of the pitch, checking the corner flags are in place, and then zigzags. Checking for the ditches, twigs, general rubbish etc and our old favourite; dogs mess. I then check the nets for stability and holes; mostly along the sides and tops. This ground is prone to foxes, so the backs of the nets usually get ripped.

I always carry tape during my warm-up so any holes can easily be closed or taped against the post. In cup games I generally get the ARs to do this, but during league games the teams provide ARs. These are generally dads, but sometimes you do get someone who knows the laws.

So with the nets taped, I check the goal area, penalty mark, and penalty area ensuring the lines are visible at both ends. If the goal area is sandy I make a note for my chat with the players.

On this bright and blustery morning Bryne management team were walking towards the pitch, talking to the League Chairman. Had they brought him to monitor the game or had they just met in the car park? With the history I have had with Bryne over the years, one could easily assume the former, however it was the latter.

Introducing yourself to the chairman can be daunting, but to move up the ladder and get appointed to prestigious games you need to get noticed for the right reasons. We talked for about 10 minutes, with him asking questions about the other games he had heard I had reffed at.

I called both teams to the middle and asked if the coaches had nominated their ARs. I introduced myself to both sides, ensuring team colours did not clash and the keepers were present, reminding them:

- To play to my whistle at all times, even if you think you have been fouled. I will deal with it. You may have advantage, and if the player isn't seriously injured I may play advantage.
- I don't tolerate back chat of any kind.
- That red and yellow cards are on the table, so let's make sure we don't use them.
- Keep elbows down when jumping for the ball.
- I don't want to see any studs in tackles.
- I don't want to see players kicking sand in the keepers face to gain advantage.
- While some of you may swear I don't want any directed at me, otherwise I may react.

I then request the managers to confirm that all players:

- Are wearing shin pads,
- Have all jewellery, including rings, removed and not taped.
- Are not wearing any spectacles or hearing aids. [If they were, I would need to discuss this further with the coach and individuals. And possibly parents too.]
- Remove all undershorts that don't match the primary short   colour.

I generally get comments on this last one, but then I remind them that they want me to abide by all the laws of the game; under short colour is one of the laws.

While the players cards are being checked, I talk with the ARs away from the players. If this was a cup game the chat would have been in the changing rooms an hour before the game, and then warm up, check the net, pitch etc together

Diary of a New Referee

For throws, I want them to tell me if the ball is in or out of play, reminding them it is the whole of the ball over the whole of the line, and to use strong flags.

Additionally...

- To use the wait and see approach for off sides. Reminding them to use a strong flag and wait for my signal. I will acknowledge the signal, but I may wave it away if the defence has advantage etc.
- All penalties to be left for me to call.
- The space between the 18 yard line and touch is their domain and I will accept anything they flag.
- For corners I want them to stand over the goal line, checking if the ball goes out during the kick or over the line for a goal. This is more important if the player is kicking with the foot closest to the goal line. Right foot on the right side, left on the left side. As there is a tendency for the ball to swing out of play before curling back into play.
- For penalties I want then on the 18 penalty / goal line intersection, looking for keeper infringements and whether the ball has crossed the goal line between the posts.

If one AR is competent, and generally they are a good standard, I ask them to take the referee whistle if I am incapacitated and cannot continue to referee.

With this and the coach's card checks complete, the captains shake hands and the ends are chosen by the winner of the coin flip. Both teams take their positions while I count the number of players, ensuring each team has a keeper present in goal. Play cannot continue until both keepers are on the field of play. The ARs take their positions, at the second last man, on the left side of the pitch, and flag to say they are ready.

So with whistle in hand and the league chairman watching, Kings kicked off. For the first 10 minutes the game has to be tight. Throw-ins have to be taken from the right place, tackles have to be crisp, with arms down etc. This sets the tone of the game and the players know what they can and cannot get away with.

Diary of a New Referee

Everything I had worked for over the last five seasons had come together, I was buzzing. I gave an indirect free kick to Bryne, and raised my arm until the ball was touched by another player. I anticipated the drop zone, keeping up with play, making sure I was within 35 feet of the ball at all times, anticipating play, making sure I was in the correct position. This way any decisions are easier to sell.

So when the Bryne striker ran in on goal, beating the midfield only to be tackled by a fantastic placed stab tackle, and then colliding with the keeper while stumbling to maintain his balance. I was in the right position, close to the incident, and crossed my arms in a scissor action to indicate no penalty.
However, the Kings keeper was injured and couldn't continue.

Play at this point had to be stopped, the ball was still in play, so I blew my whistle. The LOTG state that each team must have a keeper on the field of play. So I restarted with a dropped ball with Bryne unchallenged, passing the ball back to the Kings keeper who in turn hoofed it up the pitch.

Keeping on top of players is a man management skill, talking to the players, explaining decisions and keeping them under control. However, talking too much is not a good thing, so keep it relevant to the game.

Deep into the first half, a Bryne striker made a reckless challenge on a Kings player, I awarded a free kick. The players got up and because the Kings player didn't like the challenge he shoulder-barged the Bryne player. I was between the players within 2 steps. I asked the Bryne player to go away, as I would deal with it. I turned and gave the Kings player a verbal tongue lashing. That was all that was needed to defuse the situation.

The first half ended 0-0, and I had had a great first half, with man managing the players, keeping the throw-in inline without encroachment, and dealing with a contempt from one Kings player.

The second half started with Bryne pressurising the Kings goal. I expected the first 10 minutes to be challenging, they usually are. So I paid extra attention to tackles. So when Kings surged forward I stayed up with play, I had to be in the right place.

Diary of a New Referee

Sometimes with the speed of the game, the referee is caught out. This is why training is essential, I ran about 10 miles a week to keep fit. So when the ball shot up the pitch, I had to be in the right place on the pitch for the next phase of play. I sprinted up the pitch, running along the diagonally from right to left, aiming for the left side of the penalty area. The Kings player was fouled inches outside the penalty area, but fell into the area. I was 10 feet from the incident. He argued that he should be awarded a penalty as he was in fouled inside the penalty area. My confidence and proximity to play allowed me to sell the correct decision.

Sometimes play can change direction so fast that you can not anticipate play, so fitness is really important. The game as 1-1 going into the last few minutes. Bryne was pressuring the Kings goal. I was standing on the edge of the penalty area looking for any fouls, when Kings cleared the ball up field, I was slightly out of position. I sprinted up the field again, just outside the Bryne penalty area when Kings striker Archie blasted in the winner.

I blew my whistle and the Bryne management congratulated me on a great game. I had done it, I had finally turned Bryne on to my side. I was congratulated by the League Chairman too for a well balanced, easy to watch and extremely fair game. To top this, days later I received an email from the Bryne manager saying that he and his spectators were extremely happy with my performance. What a great Manager.

This is how I ref now, full of confidence. I know the laws and how to man manage the players, coaches and spectators. I left the field of play walking on air, full of confidence. I had upped my game bringing every aspect, every law and man management skills together to produce one of my best games. And to receive those comments was the icing on the cake.

Marking the Referee.

This section provides an guide to how referees are scored on their performance, control, decision making, communication and player management.

The first section provides an understanding of the referees overall score.

91-100 The referee was extremely accurate in decision making and very successfully controlled the game using management and communication skills to create an environment of fair play, adding real value to the game.

81-90 The referee was very accurate in decision making and successfully controlled the game using management and communication skills to create an environment of fair play.

---

71 - 80 The referee was accurate in decision making and controlled the game well, communicating with the players, making a positive contribution towards fair play.

61-70 The referee was reasonably accurate in decision making, controlled the game quite well and communicated with players, establishing a reasonable degree of fair play.

51-60 The referee had some shortcomings in the level of accuracy of decision making and control, with only limited success in communicating with the players resulting in variable fair play.

---

50 and below The referee had significant shortcomings in the level of accuracy of decision making and control with poor communication with the players which resulted in low levels of fair play

---

Diary of a New Referee

During the completion of the referees assessment form, the following points are also considered:

Control & Decision Making

- How well did the referee control the game?
- Were the players' actions recognised correctly?
- Were the Laws applied correctly?
- Were all incidents dealt with efficiently/effectively?
- Were all the appropriate sanctions applied correctly?
- Was the referee always within reasonable distance of incidents?
- Was the referee well positioned to make critical decisions, especially in and around the penalty area?
- Did the referee understand the players' positional intentions and keep out of the way accordingly?
- Did the referee demonstrate alertness and concentration throughout the game?
- Did the referee apply the use of the advantage to suit the mood and temperature of the game?
- Was the referee aware of the players' attitude to advantage?
- Did the referee use the assistants effectively?
- Did the officials work as a team, and did the referee lead and manage them to the benefit of the game?

Communication & Player Management

- How well did the referee communicate with the players during the game?
- Did the referee's level of involvement/profile suit this particular game?
- Did the referee understand the players' problems on the day – e.g. difficult ground/weather conditions?
- Did the referee respond to the changing pattern of play/mood of players?
- Did the referee demonstrate empathy for the game, allowing it to develop in accordance with the tempo of the game?
- Was the referee pro-active in controlling of the game?
- Was the referee's authority asserted firmly without being officious?

Diary of a New Referee

- Was the referee confident and quick thinking?
- Did the referee appear unflustered and unhurried when making critical decisions?
- Did the referee permit undue questioning of decisions?
- Did the referee deal effectively with players crowding around after decisions/incidents?
- Was effective player management in evidence?
- Was the referee's body language confident and open at all times?
- Did the pace off the game, the crowd or player pressure affect the referee negatively?

Final words.

I hope the examples detailed above will help you in your games to come. I am the first to put my hand up that I don't know everything. I am still learning. I just wanted to give something back to the game and help all those referee who kept asking me for guidance.

Keep going to courses run my your local county FA training officer, and if possible join a local Referee Association. It is a great opportunity to share experiences and discuss your tricky situations.

Thank you for your time.

2424623R00027

Printed in Great Britain
by Amazon.co.uk, Ltd.,
Marston Gate.